Prescription

Him

The steps you need to get you through this

breakup

Mackenzie Nall

Acknowledgments:

First, I want to thank God for loving me unconditionally and bringing me through every good and bad moment of my life. I couldn't have asked for a better father.

Second, I want to thank my mom, dad, sister, and Mike for being with me through every one of these toxic relationships. Thank you for being patient and loving me through it. I have given you guys a lot to deal with, but you still chose to stick with me. I love you all so much! I can never thank you enough.

Third, I want to thank my love, Chris Bishop. You have always been so supportive of everything I want to do. You are kind and loving and I can't thank you enough for all you do for me. Thank you for sharing in my love and letting me share in yours.

Table of Contents

Chapter 1: "I Have to Overcome This Heartbreak"

This is it – the final straw. The breaking point you've been waiting for. It's about time. I am so proud of you for making it to this point of your life! I know it's hard, and the journey has seemed long and stressful, but now you can finally start to heal. All the horrible situations that have happened to you have led to this beautiful moment of you picking up this book. Maybe you are tired of attracting the wrong men, or maybe your choice in men has practically ripped you and your loved ones apart. Whatever the situation may be, it's not too late to turn it around. Things may not be exactly what you thought they would be at this point in your life, but that's completely normal. Whether you are in your twenties, thirties, seventies, or eighties, the thing that matters most is that you are ready for change, and that is such a pivotal and powerful moment!

I've seen women who put themselves completely on the line for the men they are with and the love is not reciprocated at all. It's sad to witness and it makes me shake my head and wonder: *Why do they put up with that?* But the fact of the matter is, they don't see it from an outsider's point of view. I know you've been that woman, too. Or maybe you are the woman who is so sweet and good to your man but he cheats on you anyways. Maybe you are the woman who chose someone toxic who ripped you from everyone you loved but you still chose him over everything. Or maybe you're the woman who thinks you can fix the broken ones. Something about them makes your maternal side kick into overdrive and you love that feeling – almost like an addiction. Perhaps you always fall for the "bad boy" type because it's exhilarating to you. You would not give a good guy the time of day because they are too safe for you, which in turn is boring.

Whatever woman you identify with, even if it's all of the above, you're tired and ready for something more in life. I completely understand.

You've cried yourself to sleep too many nights. You've stayed up far too many nights wondering where he is and who he's with. You try to "be good" but you can't help but look through his phone or computer because something doesn't feel quite right to you. You snoop through his history and his text messages. You pay attention to who he looks at when you're sitting across the table from each other at a restaurant on date night. Maybe you follow him when he leaves the house. Heck, maybe you even record him talking in his sleep so you can look for clues. These are not actions that we should get comfortable doing while in a partnership. These actions stem from anxiety and trying to have control. These actions are not healthy for you or your partner in your relationship. We have to stop acting like this is a normal thing when dating someone. Dating needs to be trusting and respectful. How do you expect to grow as a couple if neither one of you can trust each other? It's a recipe for disaster.

Maybe the reason you keep going for these toxic men is because you have lost that self-confidence you need. You rely on someone else to make you feel important or loved. You look externally to find the approval that you can only get from within. I know you are probably unsure of where to start or maybe you've tried different ways before that did not work well. That's fine, don't stress out anymore. The tools I provide in this book will allow you to start taking the baby steps needed to get past this heartbreak and to move into your true, beautiful, incredible, loving self. You will gain confidence that you probably haven't had for years – if ever.

This world is full of so many angry, hurting, sad people. I believe the reason this is happening is because people are not truly dealing with themselves and their emotions. If everyone would take time daily to be with themselves and to give themselves the attention they give to everyone else, it would probably change the world in a really beautiful way. How can we expect to be loved by others when we can't even love ourselves first? What we attract is truly just a reflection of how we see ourselves and what we expect. Let that sink in. Really take a few minutes to think about the men you attract and how they treat you compared to how you see yourself.

It's a hard pill to swallow, I know. I've been in your shoes before, too. Once we are able to see things for what they are, then we can start to heal.

We are not getting any younger. Time is precious and we shouldn't waste a moment more on people who are not able to see us for the amazing women we are. This life is beautiful and exciting and full of wonderful people who will lift you up. I will lift you up. The time for lasting change is now! Make a vow to yourself that this is the day you step away from your old lifestyle and mentality and begin your new, beautiful, happy life. I would love for you to be able to get over your heartbreak once and for all. I would love to know that you have found the love you always wanted, within yourself. And even if you don't find your soulmate, you will still understand that you are fulfilled on your own.

It's time to step forward into the potential you've been throwing aside. It's time to heal your relationships with your loved ones and with yourself. It's not too late to start over. As long as you have air in your lungs, you can still admit your mistakes and move forward. You're not bound to them forever. People may try to remind you of what you were and what you did in the past, but you will know in your soul that you are not that same person. What a special feeling, knowing that whatever bad you have done or had done to you, you've moved past it even stronger than ever. The bad in your past only helped build your character and your mind.

This process will take time. It does not happen in a week or a month. You need to sit down every night or every other night and take time for your personal growth. First we have to acknowledge the mistakes and the issues we have and try to understand where they came from. Then we can start making the baby steps toward growth. Every step you take will make you stronger, even if it may not feel like it. Some days will be worse than others. You may feel like you're going backward sometimes – that's natural. It's part of your growth process. Please trust your process.

My stepson brought a tiny sunflower sprout home from school one day a few months ago. It was so small, it fit in a Dixie cup. We put it on our porch to get sun and we watered it daily. It's been exciting to see how much it grows on a daily basis. The important thing we had to do was to rotate the pot daily so the stem would not droop to one side. Instead of staking it we would rotate the pot to face the sun and the flower would draw toward the sunlight. This made the stem get stronger over time. The sunflower is now taller than our railing. We've repotted it twice so it can grow larger. This week I noticed the flower bloom coming out of the top. I was so excited! I couldn't wait to be able to see the actual flower bloom out. The reason why I'm telling you this story is because I want you to imagine yourself as that tiny stem in the Dixie cup. You are used to one way of seeing yourself and your relationships. Then, you are given sunlight and water, which helps you grow – the chapters you will read in this book. They will give your spirit the nutrients it needs to become healthy. The sunflower must be rotated daily in order to grow upright and stronger. That symbolizes you looking at things from a new perspective so you can become mentally stronger. How can you expect to grow if you only see one way of looking at the world around you? The flower needs to be re-potted as it grows. The flower can't grow larger if the pot is always small. Think of it as you needing more space. You need space to grow, so give yourself time to be alone and away from everyone. This helps you quiet your mind and give yourself a chance to talk to yourself and the universe. The stem doesn't bloom a flower as soon as it pops out of the soil. It takes the sunflower weeks to get big enough and then the flower finally blooms. That's why I say this process won't happen overnight. You will need to dedicate time to your growth process and give yourself what you need. Eventually you will bloom into the beautiful flower you were created to be. Then everyone can enjoy your true beauty. When the right one comes along, they will not pick you. They may replant you into something bigger so you can continue to grow. They will tend to you every day and make sure you have what you need to stay healthy and strong. Stop settling for these slugs who feast on your stems and leaves to make themselves stronger.

Make sure your growth process is top priority right now. This is probably one of the most important times in your life, and it needs to be taken seriously. You will not get past this if you treat it like something that can be put off until later. That time will probably never come. If you want to live your life the way you truly believe it should be, then let's make it happen. The time is now. No more making excuses. No more going back to the same old routine and the same guys. Spend time with yourself and respect yourself enough to not let others interrupt your growing process. This is your time! You have given years of yourself to these men and it's time to take it back. I know you will overcome this for good if you give yourself the chance. Fight for yourself like you fought for your ex. I promise it will be a better outcome for you. You deserve a beautiful, flourishing, happy love life with the right one. The one who is going to sweep you off your feet, treat you how you deserve to be treated, treat your loved ones well, respect you, honor you, and not control you. This life is meant to be happy, so it's time you start taking the steps needed to make that happen. Your life has so much potential to be incredible!

Chapter 2: I Understand Your Pain

By the time I was twenty-seven, I had been through a handful of failed relationships. It started out when I was nineteen and just moved to Alabama. I met a guy, fell in love, but after a few months something didn't quite feel "right" about it. I loved him the best that I could, but it seemed like the love was not reciprocated. I found myself asking him, "What's wrong?" a lot because he would be clammed up and not speaking to me. I would always blame myself for the way he acted, thinking how it was probably something I did wrong to make him act this way. I could never get the love I desired from him, which led to continuous frustration. These feelings first started happening after three months of dating and we ended up staying together for a little over a year. I kept telling myself that maybe it was just a phase or perhaps he was having a rough week or a rough month and that's why he couldn't treat me exactly how I wanted. I remember on my twentieth birthday, he didn't even get me a present. We happened to go to the mall that day and I picked up a DVD, mentioned I wanted to see it, and he bought it for me. Ta-da! That was my birthday present. We then, proceeded to go back to his house, lay on his bed, and watch some TV show about cars that I hated. He was in another one of those "clammed-up" moods and not speaking to me. I tried talking to him about why he was in such a bad mood, especially on my birthday, and he would deny everything, as always. That was the final straw for me. I got off the bed, put my shoes on, and walked out the door. He asked where I was going and I said, "I'm not staying here" with tears in my eyes. I walked out and he didn't chase after me. That's how I knew I made the right decision. I shouldn't have ever had to beg for the love I wanted. If he couldn't be bothered enough to get off the bed and come after me, then it was not meant for us to be.

A few months later I had an old friend I met online get in contact with me. We used to talk all the time in chat rooms and we always wished we could meet in person. He had a job opportunity that led him through the town I lived in and so we planned to meet up. I thought he wouldn't show because online relationships have a reputation for not working out. I was working at a sandwich shop at the time and he showed up out of nowhere. It was very surreal seeing him in person and I was overjoyed by the whole situation. He waited for me until I got off work and then we spent hours into the night talking in the parking lot. We ended up getting together officially, a long-distance relationship. We tried to see each other every weekend, taking turns traveling to each other. He gave off so many red flags but I ignored every one. I remember being at our friend's house one day on his computer and finding a file with all of his ex-girlfriends' naked photos on it. I confronted him about it and he said, "Oh, I just keep them as blackmail in case they try anything on me." Being the young and gullible girl that I was, I went right along with it. I remember it hurt me very badly, but I pushed the hurt down and went along with it because I didn't want to upset him. These instances would happen almost weekly. He would watch porn (which I have never agreed with), but I said it was okay with it because I wanted him to be happy. He sold drugs and would even drive me around in the car with his drugs without me knowing. He worked as a dish washer for a restaurant during the evening shift and sometimes would not get off until one or two in the morning. I remember the nights kept getting later and later for him to come home. One night he wasn't home until 6:30 a.m. Of course, I was never able to sleep when he was gone because my mind was wandering about what he was doing or where he was. That night I called him in a fury and asked where he was. He told me they had a corporate inspection the next day and the place had to be spotless. I didn't believe him for a second, but I said okay because I didn't want to upset him.

I have a whole laundry list of these types of situations, but I will stop myself. We lived together in Georgia for about six months and I was very unhappy. I missed my family. I told him I was moving back to Alabama to be with my family and he took it horribly. The night before I was supposed to move, he was at work again and my mind was still wandering. I remember watching TV and suddenly a voice came into my head that said, so clearly, "Check his e-mails." I immediately did and found countless e-mails between him and other women, exchanging nude photos and planning on meeting up. I was physically sick. My blood was boiling and my body was shaking with rage. I called my mom crying hysterically and told her what happened. She said she would come help me move the next morning and to just stay there and be calm. I called him, screaming, and let him know I found his e-mails. He was apologetic and said he wouldn't come home that night. I thought seriously about trashing his whole house and throwing his TV out the window, but his mother was a lawyer and I knew better than to get myself into that. As the night progressed, he called me again and told me he was sitting in his car in someone's driveway with a gun in his mouth. He told me he felt horrible and he wanted to die. Of course, I was furious, but I still had to console him so that he would not go through with it. I spent the rest of those morning hours trying to talk him out of it. He turned the situation around to be all about him again. That relationship was extremely emotionally abusive and hard to overcome. He was a pathological liar, among other things, as it turned out. I spent a few months drinking and crying myself to sleep at my friend's apartment. I could not seem to get over what he had done to me and my friends were getting tired of seeing me as a drunken mess on their bathroom floor.

A few months passed and I had met the last abusive man I would love, James. We met at a party at my friend's place and didn't think much of each other. He started hanging out with us every night at the apartment and he easily became an installation to our close friends group. We got to know each other better and soon after, we began dating. Our relationship was great, or so I thought. We would have our fights every once and a while, but what couple doesn't? Over time, our friend group started having a lot of drama and people were slowly dwindling away. We thought we had figured out who the culprit of the drama was. Then James started telling me what the people in my circle were saying about me behind my back. I stopped hanging out at the apartment as much. James came to live with me. I was sharing a house with my sister and her husband. The months went by and I began noticing a lot of chaos within my family as well. James would tell me things that my sister and her husband would say behind my back. I was getting really frustrated with all the drama happening and I confronted my family about what they had said. My family denied it all, which made me even angrier. I started becoming very detached from my family and soon, I stopped going to see my friends at all. I cut all ties with them because I was tired of being talked about in a negative way. The turmoil got to be too much at my house, so me and James got our own apartment with one of his friends. We lived together for about five months and it was pretty rocky. We started fighting more and I would catch him in lies all the time. One night he said he was going to the gym. Once he had been gone a few minutes, I got in my car and went to the gym he was registered at. He wasn't there. I went straight home and waited for him. When he got back, he was still in his jeans and shirt. I asked him why he wasn't sweaty and he said he had taken a shower at the gym because he sweated through his clothes working out. He then proceeded to get in our shower. While he was in there, I got his gym clothes out of the hamper to see if they were wet. They weren't. They even still smelled like dryer sheets. We got into a huge fight when he got out of the shower and I confronted him about it. I broke up with him a few days later. If he was lying about something as simple as going to the gym, what else was he lying about? We broke up for two months, but we still worked together, which made it hard not to stay in contact. We tried to start over during those couple months and take it slow. We got back together in November 2015 and things seemed great. We were even shopping for engagement rings and planning to get married in 2016.

One night we were at work together and I was passing the nightly snacks out to our patients. I came around the corner and he was on the phone talking quietly. He motioned to me to be quiet and then whispered "it's my mom." I said okay and kept walking around to the other side of the building. That same clear voice came back into my head and said, "You need to stop and listen to what he's saying." I did. I walked back a few steps so I could hear, and he was talking to a girl about the night they had together. I remember he said "What we had together was purely sexual. I don't want to be a home-wrecker." They continued to whisper but I had heard enough. I came around the corner and asked who it was. He continued to act like it was his mother and he got off the phone. We got into a huge argument and the last thing I remember he said it was someone who worked with us, a nurse who was engaged. My vision went red and I slapped him in the face as hard as I could. He ducked, so he didn't get it too bad, unfortunately. I ran out of my job sobbing. It all made sense though. The drama within my friend group, the "trash talking" that my friends were doing behind my back, the chaos within my family causing us to move out – it was all because of James. He was the puppeteer controlling everyone. He would tell me lies about my friends and then tell my friends lies about me. That's what caused us to stop being friends. He did the same things within my family, telling them I was saying things that I wasn't and vice versa. He manipulated and lied so much that it tore me from everyone I loved. He isolated me all to himself and then cheated on me to top it all off. The damage he caused within my family was something we had to overcome for a while. I still have not seen my friends since this all happened. We all moved and went our separate ways. James was a narcissist and I had no idea. He would turn arguments around to make them always seem like everyone else's fault. I had so many trust issues after I left him.

Breaking up with James was such a huge step. From that moment forward I was done with being in relationships. I took a hard look at myself and I knew that I was the common denominator in my failed relationships. I had to find out what in me was causing these guys to think they could treat me this way. I spent the entire year of 2016 alone. If I wasn't at work or at school, then I was in my room by myself. I had to move in with my mom and stepdad because I had just started nursing school and I would not be able to work much. Thankfully they agreed to help me get through school. I didn't spend much time with them at all, though. They were understanding and let me have my time alone. I cried myself to sleep for months. 2016 was the most life-changing year for me. I needed that alone time to finally understand my deep-seated issues and how to get past them. I dealt with my problems that I had been suppressing for over a decade. That year taught me who I really was and who I really wanted to become. I took up meditation and listened to motivational sermons and speakers constantly. I studied for school and in my spare time I studied the things I found interesting. I spent a lot of time on my back porch, looking out into the woods, enjoying the rain, or staring at birds. I allowed myself to be with me and to be with God. Those are the two most beneficial relationships you could ever develop. After almost a decade of abusive, unfulfilling relationships, I had finally come to my breaking point. Thank God for that. Journaling became a really big outlet for me, as well as painting and meditation. I started blogging to document my progress through the year and what all I had learned. It's beautiful to go back and read the beginning journal entries compared to the progressive blog entries I was writing.

This book is packed full of my top solutions to overcome situations like these. I'm sure you've also been through something similar – probably more than once. That's why you're reading this. 2016 changed my life because I had finally reached my end. This is your year. You've reached your end and you are ready to move forward once and for all so that you can lead the life you want to live. You deserve to be happy, prosperous, and to find the right one for you. We have to deal with ourselves first, though, in order to progress. That's why it hasn't worked yet. The time has come. This is it.

Chapter 3: How Do I Heal?

"The cure for pain is in the pain."

— Rumi

In this book you will be given the steps needed to not only overcome your heartbreak, but to understand what caused it so that you can avoid those contributors in the future. There's no point in getting over our heartbreak if we don't understand what to avoid so that we don't repeat the same process. This book will break it down for you and make it easy to understand and relate to. I will ask questions to get your thought process going as well. It may be tough to deal with sometimes, but by the end of the book you will feel like a new woman.

In Chapter 4, we will explore is how to embrace our pain. Nobody likes this step, and that's understandable. I didn't like it at the time either, but it's such a huge step in the healing process. It doesn't feel good, but we can't keep ignoring this key part of the problem. How are we expected to grow from anything if we don't experience the pain and acknowledge what it taught us? This is not the time to continue ignoring the hurt that has happened to you. Let's see it for what it is, experience this emotion, and learn from it so it will make us stronger. Just like going to the gym, you have to feel the burn and the pain. It may be sore for a few days afterward, too, but every time you will get stronger. When you look back at yourself as you went through this time, you will be so proud.

Thinking positively is the next detail we will discuss in Chapter 5. For me, positive thinking is what has gotten me through some of the hardest times in my life. Life can be really rough sometimes. Why make it worse by thinking nothing but negative thoughts? That's like adding salt to your wound. Not everyone is an optimist, but during this period it's very important to keep your mind full of positive thoughts and moments of happiness. This is what will keep you moving forward even when it gets the worst. Having a negative, angry environment can hinder evolvement. This is the time in your life where you really need to take your progress seriously and move on from this for good. Don't let your negative mindset stunt your growth.

Moving on to Chapter 6, we will discuss how to create a healthy environment that will help you flourish. Do you have a place in your house or near you that you can escape to on a daily basis? Many of us don't. That's the purpose for this chapter. I'm going to go over how you can find a space, make it your own, and fill it will inspiration and things that make you happy. It's a lot more difficult to grow as a person when you don't have a place of escape. Things get chaotic all around us, so we really need to create a beautiful, happy, inspirational place to be. Hopefully you can be in this place daily for at least a few hours. If not, I want you to try to be here once daily, even if it's for a few minutes. This will be a place of reflection for you. It will be a place where you can get quiet and talk to yourself, a place to be real with yourself. Think of it as your "happy place." My happy place used to be my back porch. That's where I did most of my growing. It was quiet and peaceful. I got to watch the birds and lizards. I would take naps on the couch and listen to the wind chimes. It was a haven for me. I want you to be able to find a wonderful place like that so you can explore your mind without interruption.

In Chapter 7, we will talk about how to understand ourselves better. We will explore the reasons why we make the decisions we make. Why we choose these men who ultimately end up hurting us. We will go back to our roots and discover what happened when we were younger that set the tone for these unhealthy relationships. Not only that, we will try to understand the reasons why we behave the way we do and why we think the thoughts we think. Most of us have had something bad happen to us in our lives. A lot of us choose to push the hurt down deep and ignore it. Then the issues from that bad thing bubble up to the surface in other ways, like toxic relationships or bad behaviors. You may think you have it under control by pushing it down, but it will shine through in some aspect of your life if you don't deal with it. This is why we keep this cycle of breakups. This is also why we view ourselves in a negative way or think unhealthy, negative thoughts. We don't just get the way we are by chance – it takes years of suppressing our issues to bring us to this point. This chapter is a tough one, because most people don't want to revisit the bad things that happened in the past. We want to ignore it because it hurts so badly. But in order to understand why we are the way we are, and why we keep making these bad choices, we have to get to the roots of the issue. It will probably get messy and painful but keep pushing through and get some understanding from it. Don't let your pain go without purpose. Once you recognize the patterns of these self-destructing behaviors, then we can more easily see them if they start to happen again in the future. You will be able to stop it in its tracks and choose a better path to take.

Chapter 8 will be about rewiring your thoughts. Maybe it's hard for you to keep a good attitude because you've never really done it before. In this chapter I will explain some ways to help you to turn your negative thoughts into positive ones. Not only will you learn how to change your negativity, but you will also learn how to see yourself in a new way. You will be able to turn the tables on the negative situations in your life. Your mind is such a powerful tool. You can choose to have it work to your advantage or you can continue the same thoughts you have been thinking. Maybe the way you've been thinking is not just hurting you, but maybe it's hurting the people around you as well. They might be tired of hearing your negative self-talk and having to try to make you feel better. Maybe they are tired of hearing the same sad stories you tell. We have to get control of our minds and the way we look at things so that we don't run everyone off who loves us. Our thoughts create our reality. If your thoughts are constantly self-destructive then how do you expect your reality to be any different? We will go over how to see the thoughts that tear you and others down and how we can think of things in a new perspective. This will help you see the world in a whole new light.

In Chapter 9 we take a look inward – and it's one of my favorites. This was probably the biggest lesson I learned in my lifetime. If you are like most others, you probably seek love from a boyfriend, a mother, father, sibling, etc. You yearn for that approval and uplifting affirmation. When we break up with one person we might wait a month until someone new comes along and we couple up again. It's as if we can't just be alone with ourselves. This is why we are forever stressed out or in some type of turmoil. We keep seeking outward approval when we really need to look for that approval within ourselves. Yes, I know the feeling of love is wonderful, but you are completely capable of giving it to yourself. You don't have to find it in others. Don't keep putting a band aid on the situation by going from one breakup into another relationship right away. It will never give you the satisfaction and approval you are looking for. You will continue to be disappointed. Once you love yourself the way you want to be loved, it will shine so bright and people will see it. You might attract the right one once you understand this lesson.

Keep practicing! Chapter 10 will explain the necessity of practicing what you learn. Once you learn the lesson doesn't mean you have it forever. Sometimes you might forget and fall back into an old routine. That's perfectly normal. When it happens, just get this book out and skim through it or read it over again if you feel the need. As long as you are growing, then you're doing well. Don't stay stagnant. Keep growing forward.

Chapter 11 will overview why things may have not been working for you in the past as well as what may continue to go wrong if you don't decide to make a change. I truly believe this life is supposed to be happy, fun, exciting, and full of love. I believe everyone deserves true love. Even the meanest people out there did not get that way just because they felt like it. People have bad things happen to them and they learn to adapt in whatever way possible. It doesn't mean they have to be this way forever. It doesn't mean they are not worthy of this wonderful, happy life, and true love. No matter what type of person you may be, I want you to find peace in yourself and to find the love you've been seeking so much. You deserve to be happy. It's time you make the changes you need and give yourself the life that the world may have tried to take away from you.

It may seem like a lot, but these lessons are straightforward and full of life-changing material. I don't want to waste your time with nonsense, I just want to give you the steps needed to make a positive impact on your life forever. I'm tired of seeing so many hurting people in this world. I've been one of those people for far too long. I broke the cycle for myself and I strive to do that for as many people as I possibly can. I believe if we all take responsibility for our own personal growth, the world would be such a happier place. We can't go out and expect to change the world if we don't change ourselves first. Your life has so much potential, it's time to live up to it.

Chapter 4: Embracing Your Pain

Yes, you read that correctly. I know it seems completely bizarre, but it's a huge step. I know you are probably thinking, "How does leaning into the pain help make the pain go away?" Well, pain helps us to grow. Think of this period of time as your "growing pains" period. It seems so horrible at the time, but when you look back on it you will understand just what a beautiful process it really is, and without it, you could have never became what you are now.

It seems like our society these days just expects to feel good all the time. We are constantly bombarded with social medial that shows people's life high points. We see people on TV and in magazines who are stunning and rich and have everything going for them. We listen to gurus who tell us that we must be happy all the time and not focus on the pain in our own lives or in others. It's only natural to think that we should have it together every moment of every day. The majority of our world uses substances or things to numb them whenever they begin to feel any pain. Got a headache? Take a pill. Depressed? Take another pill. Stressed out? Drink some alcohol. Feeling insecure? Sleep with that person tonight. Need energy? Snort that powder. Bored? Do all of it in the same evening.

This is such a sad thing to witness. For some reason people cannot fathom dealing with themselves. I believe that's why our world has gotten in the shape it's in. People are dying of overdoses every minute of every day and the statistics keep rising. Maybe if we all took time to be alone for a bit every day or a couple times a week just so we can work on ourselves, this world would probably be so much better off.

Pain is just a normal human emotion. If you are on this earth breathing air then you will experience a vast array of emotions. We can deal with almost all of them but for some reason we can't seem to wrap our heads around pain. Why is this?! Pain is just as important an emotion as any other. We have to honor it and experience it too. Without pain we would not be able to learn. Imagine if you put your hand on a hot stove eye when you were young and burned yourself severely. Can you imagine if you didn't learn from that horrible pain you felt? You would probably do it multiple times in your life if you didn't feel that terrible pain and understand what a bad idea that was. Thank God for pain! Now, I'm not saying we need to go looking for pain so that we can learn more lessons. Masochism is not recommended. The point is, we must take the time to feel the pain and understand what went wrong so that we can learn and move forward.

Have you been numbing your pain with anything? Think for a few minutes about what you have been doing to ignore the sadness or discomfort you feel from your breakups, or anything bad in your life. Do you shop? Gamble? Sleep around? Do drugs or get drunk as a skunk? Find another relationship as soon as you're out of one? Write down what it is you do to escape it and acknowledge it. Have you been doing this cycle with every breakup you've had? You have a boyfriend, break up with each other, and then you immediately numb the pain because it's too unbearable or uncomfortable to deal with? If you don't deal with this pain then you will never learn from it and this cycle will continue! You can't keep numbing yourself and then expect this issue to go away. It will just keep recycling until you finally deal with it. Please, just sit in your pain for however long it takes to get over it. For some, it will be a couple months or maybe even less. For others, it could be a year or more. It just depends on each person's situation. Don't beat yourself up for how long it's taking to get through the pain.

When James and I broke up, I remember crying myself to sleep for months. Then it started being only a couple nights a week. It dwindled down as time went on and I began to find my happiness again. Give yourself however long you need to get over it without numbing yourself. Do not be ashamed of your process. Don't let people tell you that you need to "quit crying and get over him." You take your time and do it right the first time so that you can grow strength and confidence. Trust your unique process.

This time in your life will probably feel so messy and horrible, which is totally fine. Sometimes life is messy and horrible, but it is only temporary. Don't think that you will be in this forever. This time in your life is actually very beautiful and transformational. All the terrible things that have happened have led you to this incredible moment of new beginnings! Even though you may be ugly crying right now, just remember that this process is beautiful. You are healing. Let your emotions out. Journal about them. Write a private blog. Paint. Dance. Sing. Exercise. Watch chick flicks. Whatever it is that will help you get your feelings out instead of bottling them up or numbing them. Do what feels right in this time of discomfort.

I know it sounds crazy, but thank the universe for bringing you to this pivotal time in your life. Thank God for helping you through the transformation and the sadness. Even if you can't see the light right now, just keep faith that you will make it through. Envision yourself, healed, confident, happy.... Focus on that beautiful vision of yourself whenever you feel depressed or upset. Understand that you are on the exact path you're supposed to be to become that incredible woman. You are on your way to her, so be proud of yourself. She's eagerly waiting for you with open arms. You have all the tools you need to grow in this pain and to reach your goals. Go ahead and give yourself a pat on the back or a kiss in the mirror.

The tears may continue to flow. It's only natural. Maybe you are not just dealing with this breakup, but also the previous breakups you've been through. Maybe you never dealt with those pains. You might even be dealing with things that were done to you in the past that have nothing to do with breakups. That's perfectly fine too. Whatever pain you may be feeling, this is a great time to see it for what it is and to move on from it. Aren't you so tired of pushing this stuff down? It gets exhausting to always act like you're fine and nothing bothers you. It's tiring to always be "the strong one" who can pick herself up and go on about her life as if nothing happened. I know you feel like you need to put on a brave face, but it's okay to be human and have emotions. It's so necessary to let them out. You don't have to be a cry baby in front of people, but you also don't have to be ashamed of saying "I need time to heal." People need to respect your process, and if they don't then you might need to distance yourself for a while. Love yourself and be gentle with yourself.

This process will most likely get ugly. It's necessary. In order to truly heal and move forward you *must* let yourself feel these pains. You will probably be lying in your floor ugly crying with snot bubbles coming out of your nose, sobbing until your chest hurts. Just when you think you have calmed down, here comes another wave of sadness and sobbing. This may happen several days a week for a while. You have to sit in it and understand it. Why are you crying so hard? Is it because you feel alone or inadequate? Is it because you feel like a failure? Do you feel thrown away? Do you feel sorry for yourself because you don't have what your best friend has? Whenever you feel this pain or whenever you have a sob spell, take time to write down what you are feeling in the moment. There's no point in crying all the time if you don't take note of your thought process. You have to begin to notice what it is that's causing the pain. This will help you recognize it and work through it. Maybe you will start to notice trends in what triggers your tears. I cried because I couldn't figure out what was so bad about me that made men want to treat me the way they did. It wasn't just James – it was all my breakups. I felt so inadequate. I felt like dirt on the bottom of someone's shoe. Obviously, there was something wrong with me that made me not able to keep a man. I had to recognize these thought patterns and turn them around to what I wanted. I began telling myself the opposite of what I would think – redirecting my thoughts (which we will discuss more in Chapters 5 and 8). Once I started exploring where my pain was coming from, I was able to move forward and get through it.

Maybe you have never heard this before, but I am so proud of you. This is such a huge step in the right direction for you. To pick up this book and make a conscious effort to break this toxic cycle in your life is an incredible thing to do. It's easy to continue to find men who aren't good for you, but they feel good at the time. It's so easy to not try to grow. People love to stay in their comfort zones, but you decided to break the chains. For that, I am so extremely proud of you! You are such a warrior! Take some time to reflect on your beautiful self and the things you are doing to improve your life. Even if it's just one or two things- the fact that you are making any effort at all is wonderful. You are doing better than many people in the world. Give yourself some love and attention and don't ignore these emotions.

Eventually, things will start to get easier. You will wake up and start to look forward to your daily progress. I told you about how I would cry myself to sleep for a few months after breaking up with James. Then it eased up after a while. Eventually I was able to go weeks without crying. I would tend to my own growth every day. After a month or so I really started enjoying my time alone. At first, it was painful being completely secluded, but after I started to heal, I cherished my time alone. I would have date night with myself once a week. I would take myself shopping or go get a pedicure. I would meditate and spend time in nature alone. I would paint or dance by myself. Those were some of the best days of my life. I remember sitting in my nursing lecture one day and being so excited because it was Tuesday which meant it was "Kenzie date night." I looked forward to being with myself. What a powerful feeling, to know that you will be happy even if you're alone. I would not have gotten to that point if I didn't embrace my pain and work through it. I sat in it for as long as my spirit needed to get through it. I'm so thankful I took time to be alone and to understand my pain and where it was coming from. It helped me learn so much about myself. I continued to keep the faith and envision my future self. That kept my head above the water. It was hard to see the light at the time, but looking back, it was one of the biggest growing experiences of my life. I will always be thankful for it.

I know, I know, I know – it sucks right now. I know it's messy and hard and you can't understand the point of the pain right now. Please just trust me that it is necessary. There's no point in having all this pain in your life if you don't use it to your advantage. Do not let this pain go without purpose! Trust your process and deal with yourself. You will thank yourself in the end.

Chapter 5: Positive Thinking?

Yes, this probably sounds totally cliché, but it's the truth. Positive thinking is extremely important in any stage of your life. It's what makes or breaks us. Have you ever known someone who – no matter how bad things get – always stays calm and has such a good, positive energy about themselves? Now think of the opposite person you know. Someone who – no matter how good things are – always has a problem for every solution. Which person do you think gets ahead more in life?

Positivity is like a life-raft in troubled waters. It helps us stay afloat even when we feel like we might die. There will be many rough days during your healing process, that's guaranteed. This does not mean you're doing it wrong and it doesn't mean you need to stop and turn around. Keep swimming through those waves of despair and use positive thinking as a life-raft.

Some days you will feel like you are going through the motions. You will keep telling yourself, "I'm smart, beautiful, loved, and loving. I am worthy of happiness and true love" but you will not feel like it's the truth. This is completely normal as well. Sometimes positive thinking is just faking it till you make it. You might not feel it for a long time but then one day something in you will snap. You will wake up and feel special and worthy. You will understand how powerful you are. For some of you it may come gradually. Each day you might wake up feeling a little more beautiful than the day before. Maybe you start sticking up for yourself in bad situations more often or stop apologizing constantly. Whatever may happen, just trust the process and know it's perfect for you.

It's so important that we monitor what goes on within our heads. As women, all we see around us is how we are "supposed" to look or act or smell or be. This makes it extremely hard for us to accept our reality and what we were born with. It's a shame that this world makes us feel so unworthy. Just because they shove it in our faces doesn't mean we have to accept it. We have to be our own best friend, our own cheerleader. No, I may not look like the models in the magazines and I may not be a fantasy like the women in porn, but it has nothing to do with my worth and what I deserve from life. I am perfect just as I was made and so were you. We are all worthy of happiness and genuine love. When you start comparing yourself to others, that's when the anxiety and depression kicks in. Comparison steals joy. Please, be mindful of the thoughts you are thinking because that creates the energy you put out.

If you are living in an inward state of comparison, anxiety, unworthiness, shame, lack, then that's the energy you give off. In turn, you will find people who feed on those weaknesses or people who feel the same as you. These are not healthy relationships. Can you recall a time when maybe a group of girls you knew would get together and talk trash about other girls not in their circle? These girls hang out with each other because they are all insecure and feel the need to speak badly of others in order to lift themselves up. Or maybe a religious person who constantly bashes you for doing something that is considered a sin. That person might feel the need to constantly point out that flaw in you because they secretly have that flaw within themselves and it makes them uncomfortable to see it. I want you to take a few minutes and think about the people closest to you. Write down what traits they have that may not be ideal. Now, think about whether or not you see those traits within yourself. Most likely, many of you will have at least a few that you can relate to. This is not a fun exercise, but it is necessary. It's important to see how our thought process influences the world we live in.

I work at a drug and alcohol detox center as a nurse part time. I remember a few months ago a woman came to treatment who was very hypersexual with the men, very dramatic and attention seeking, bullied the other women, and was defiant among our staff. She was a very difficult patient to treat but she stayed the entire 35 days. One day she was having to meet with the CEO and director of nursing (again) for not following the rules and being disruptive among the community. Our director asked her, "Do you notice that chaos follows you?" and she said "Yes." The director said: "You are the common denominator of the chaos. You need to see that you bring this upon yourself." Of course, the patient was livid and caused a scene. A couple days later, she came back to the director and admitted that in that moment, she finally realized that she was causing the chaos. She said it was a huge lesson to learn but she was thankful the director said it. This patient was attracting all this drama because her thoughts were so chaotic and negative. She was always seeking outward attention, whether it be sexual attention from the men, negative/abusive attention from the women, or defiance within our staff. She still struggled with it throughout the rest of her stay, but I believe it helped her see a part of herself she had never noticed before. Once we see that part of ourselves then we can start trying to make it better.

Be mindful of the thoughts you think. Start to notice how many negative thoughts you have within a day. Once you notice, then start making an effort to reword your thoughts. You may look in the mirror after your shower and think, "Gosh, I am such a cow!" but you can reword that thought to be "I see myself exactly as I am, and I choose to love me." That is such a beautiful thing to do for your spirit. The world is critical and mean enough – you need to speak kindly to yourself. Understand that you will always be a work in progress, constantly evolving. Think about how special that is. You never have to settle on how you are *now*. You will be different by this time next year. Make a conscious effort to improve instead of getting worse or staying the same.

If you can find one thing to see in a positive light every day, your life will start to change. Even if it's the smallest circumstance, like your bread landing jelly side up on the kitchen floor- it will keep unfolding until all you see are positive situations. Traffic becomes a way for God, the universe, whatever you believe to protect you from an accident that may have happened. Your hot water heater breaking triggers you to appreciate that you have much more. Your car breaks down on the way to work causing you to stop the busyness, sit in your car, and look at the beautiful trees around you. Maybe your father falls ill and you haven't spoken to him in 15 years, but his illness causes you two to hash things out once and for all before he leaves this earth. Every situation has a positive and negative light. It's like two sides of the same coin. Decide which one you would rather focus on. Positivity is much more productive in the long run.

Probably one of the main negative thoughts you are thinking right now in your life is, "I have another failed relationship to add to my list" or "I am so embarrassed about this breakup, I can't even go in public." I know it's hard to think otherwise. Please, don't ever be ashamed of your breakup. Be proud of yourself that you did not stay in a toxic environment just to keep your reputation shiny among others. People will *always* have negative things so say, no matter how perfect you are. You might as well live your life the way you want and be in a healthy environment. Be kind to yourself. Know that what you did was necessary. Maybe you didn't even break off the relationship. Maybe it was them – either way, you can move forward, and I am so proud of you for that.

We are all doing the best we can with what we know right now. Don't look back on yourself and get angry with your decisions or how you acted. Likely, you were just doing the best you could at the time. Nobody on this earth goes into a situation with expectations to do the worst they can. You must forgive yourself for the past so you can move on from it. Not forgiving yourself will cause you to not grow. This is such a necessary part of your growth process. What's done is done and nothing can change the past, so you might as well quit beating yourself up over it. It's completely counter-productive. Just remember, this is the first day of the rest of my life. You will continue to do the best you can, I'm sure. Stop stressing yourself out about what can't be changed.

When I was going through my breakup with James, it was very depressing. I cried all the time and I couldn't make sense of things. My mind would reel over what went wrong and how I could have done better. I would sit in my room and my thoughts would spiral out of control down this rabbit hole. The day would be lost to nothing but negative thoughts. I eventually started going outside on my back porch when I would get into these spells. I would sit on my comfy couch on the screened in porch and just stop my mind from thinking anything. I started noticing birds and wildlife once I stopped the negative thoughts. I would focus all my attention on that bird sitting on the fence. I would imagine what the bird might be thinking or how it looked up close. I would focus on its colors and how it chirped a conversation with other birds. I made up the dialogue in my head. This completely brought me out of that negative thought spiral I was in. Even though I wasn't necessarily thinking "positive" thoughts, at least I wasn't thinking negatively. Focusing on something outdoors would always help me reconnect. I started spending every afternoon on my back porch thinking about nothing but what was in front of me. My back porch became my sanctuary. That's the place where I grew the most. Sunshine or stormy rain, I was there every day.

Positive thinking may seem easier said than done, I understand. I urge you to make a daily conscious effort to find something happy in whatever comes your way. You may have depression right now that feels debilitating. Just remind yourself every day "This is only temporary. It will not last forever." Keep saying it until it happens. Some days will feel like you are right back to square one- this is totally normal. Don't beat yourself up about it! Trust that this is part of your process and it's okay. Tomorrow will probably be better. If it's not, then maybe next week will be. You will think the tears are all dried up and then one night the floodgates will open. You will be frustrated because you thought you were past that. It's just part of your process. Try not to get frustrated with yourself and start the negative self-talk again. Please don't derail any of the progress you've made just because you have a tough day. If you sense you are having a bad day and you feel like you're back at the beginning, thank the universe for this process. Thank God for bringing you through everything up to this point and for continuing to guide you through the rest of the lessons. Trust that it will get better and you are becoming stronger. I kept a prayer journal through 2016. I remember most days would be entries trying to find good things to thank him for. There were a couple days that I actually let God have it. I said everything except cuss words, and I was mad as a hornet when I was writing. I understand that those moments were necessary for me to move forward, though. I had to get it out in order to keep going. You will have moments like these too, and it's okay! Don't be angry with yourself. It's perfect.

Expect greatness for yourself. Really and truly meditate on the person you want to be. Get a clear vision of yourself in the near future. How will you look? How will you hold yourself? How will you dress, smell, act, smile? Will you have more confidence or more of a beautiful glow around you? Get very specific about it and bring it up into your daily life. If you see a nice car on the street, picture that woman in it. If you see a happy old married couple, imagine you and your future lover in their place. Picture yourself eating at a café alone and being completely content with yourself. Imagine yourself in that career you desire and doing a wonderful job. How can the universe give you what you desire if you don't even know what that is? Surround yourself with people who lift you up and make you grow. Get away from these people who drag your mentality back into the gutters. Negative people will want to hold you in their mindset. You must break free from these people and strive for more. Even if it means being alone, that's better company than around people who will drain the happiness and hope from you. Do what's best for you right now because that's exactly what you need. Take care of your spirit and your mentality. Like I said, this is such a powerful time in your life, and you must take control of your growth. Love yourself enough to put you above all others right now. It's tough to do sometimes, but it will benefit you and everyone around you in the end.

Chapter 6: I Need Space

"Peace can be a lens through which you see the world. Be it. Live it.

Radiate it out. Peace is an inside job."

— Dr. Wayne Dyer

Do you have a place in your house or around your neighborhood you could go and spend time alone? Do you have a place that brings you peace that is away from others? Many people don't. This makes it so hard to be able to have time to yourself to think and to escape from the chaos around you. No wonder you are so stressed out! If you have no place of solitude, it can really take a toll on your mental health.

Try to find an area preferably in a place you spend a lot of time at, like home. Make it somewhere you can have access to every day. Try to spend at least a few hours in this area every day if possible. The more time you spend alone, the more chances you will have to talk to yourself, observe your thoughts, and to understand yourself on a deeper level. Make this place quiet, comfortable, and welcoming. Let it be somewhere that people aren't coming in and out of. You do not want to be disrupted in this time of self-reflection.

It's important to fill this space with things that inspire you and make you happy. Print out inspirational quotes and pin them all over the walls. Create a vision board of what you want from life. If you don't know what a vision board is, basically it's a poster board that represents whatever you want in life. You can cut pictures out of magazines, print photos you find online, type words or quotes and paste them to this board. The key is to imagine what your life would be like if it was completely perfect and you had everything you ever wanted. Put this vision board somewhere that you will easily see it every day. It's like subliminal messaging for your mind. If you glance at it once or twice every day your mind will continue to work toward getting what is on the board. Keep surrounding yourself with things that bring inspiration and happiness. If you love flowers, then make a point to keep fresh flowers in this space at all times. Incorporate scents that bring you back to happy times in your life. Maybe focus on keeping different aromatherapy items nearby.

My bedroom was another quiet space I loved to be in. If I wasn't on my back porch, I was in my bedroom. I had two vision boards posted in front of my bed. I had inspirational quotes taped to my mirror. I always had candles burning and aromatherapy lotions at my bedside. I made sure I had comfortable bedding and soft lighting. I kept a TV in my room so I could watch chick flicks and eat ice cream in bed on my "Kenzie date nights." I even had a maternity full-body pillow that I would use to meditate on. My bedroom was so relaxing, and I always looked forward to getting home to it. Even to this day, my apartment is still filled with these wonderful things. Now, it's not just my bedroom, it's my entire living space that is peaceful. I have a tiny balcony that only fits two chairs, but any empty space on the floor or ceiling is filled with flowers and plants. It's nice looking out my sliding glass doors and seeing nothing but green plants, flowers, and birds despite living in an apartment complex. Your space is what you make it.

Not only can you create a peaceful space like this, you can also incorporate things that bring you happiness back into your life. Are there things that you did years ago that would make you feel so joyful, but as time went on you lost track? I started painting in high school and it became such a huge part of my life as time went on. When I was in my early 20s my entire bedroom from floor to ceiling was covered in different paintings I had done. I loved it so much. As I got older, I stopped doing it as much because I was working more and getting more involved in these toxic relationships. Eventually I hadn't done it in years. Once I broke up with James, I started painting again. It was such a great feeling when I started back. It brought me back to the times that I wasn't concerned about all the nonsense that I was worried about now. Not only did I start painting, but I started dancing again also. Not professionally or on a team, but I did it in my mirror when I was alone. It was almost like I was remembering who I was again. I was acknowledging the parts of me that made me special. Through the years, these guys had put pressure on me to become something I wasn't and to put on a mask. Imagine someone coming in and covering up a beautiful stone wall with paint. Throughout the years a different person would come in and paint it what color they thought it needed to be in order to be beautiful. Eventually the coats of paint become so thick and disgusting. Once I broke up with James and spent time alone, I felt like I was scrubbing all those layers of paint off, and I could finally be that beautiful stone wall I was meant to be. It may seem like a funny comparison, but it gets the point across. No more letting people make us the way they think we should be! We were created exactly how we were supposed to be, and it's beautiful. It's time to sand down those layers and get back to our original self. Let's do more things that bring us back to those times that we felt the most like ourselves. Strive to do one thing – no matter how little – that will make you feel that joy again every day.

When you are not alone, it's important to surround yourself with people who are uplifting. This peaceful space needs to follow you even outside of the home. When you are at work, find people who aren't into the drama, find people who don't talk trash about others. Always strive to be better. If you surround yourself with people who are kind, uplifting, or people who are successful and good, then you will automatically start to rise to their level. If you continue to surround yourself with the same people who are negative, then you will not grow. You can't expect to advance your mentality if you are still surrounded by the same situations you have been in. Find new friends who will be a good influence on you. Someone who will invite you to breakfast and ask you how your life is going instead of someone who will invite you to the club and rant about how horrible their boyfriend is. You may be thinking, "Well, maybe if I become more positive then I can uplift them into a new way of thinking." That's a sweet thought and believe me, I have been there too. Right now, we are trying to get *you* better – not your friends. We have to make you stronger and put you on a new level first. And honestly, you can try to change the people around you because you love them, but it will never work. People will only change when they want to. They may get a little better for a few months, but then they will sink right back into their old ways and leave you so disappointed.

At the beginning of this book I told you about how I lost my friends and still don't speak to them, mainly because James tore us apart. But another reason why I chose not to rekindle my relationship is because they were not growing – specifically my best friend, Adam. When I moved to Alabama when I was nineteen I met Adam at the place I was working. He was totally opposite from me. Tall, robust, gay man who smoked like a chimney and drank like a fish. He was cynical and witty, and he was always cracking me up. I was short, tiny, and always happy and positive. We got along great. Throughout the years he always stayed the same. He was mad about something every day of his life, even if it was tiny. I was always trying to make him see the bright side of life. After years of doing this I became exhausted. He would do well for a while and then he would slip back into his old ways. As time went on, it actually got worse. During the end of my relationship with James he was drinking more and having trouble with his finances. I tried to help all I could but it got to the point that he did not want to help himself.

He was unemployed at that time and I had been trying to help find him a job. His friends and I would loan him money so he could pay his bills. I remember going to his apartment one day and I told him about a fast food place just across the street from his apartment that was hiring. He said "No, that place is dirty." I said "Well, maybe with you working there you could make it clean again." And he kept refusing. I got so infuriated with him. I grabbed my things, walked out the door, and never went back. I had been trying so hard to help him out of the situation he was in, but he would not budge. I was done with trying to change his life. This is why I am so adamant about you helping yourself right now, and not anyone else. You cannot keep putting your own growth on hold so that your friends or family can come with you. People will change when they are ready to. You are ready to change right now, which is why you are reading this book and they aren't. Give yourself honor and do what is right for you. You can try to pull someone out of their hole for years and years, but you will never pull them out. You think you are saving them by jumping in the hole to help them out, but then you both get stuck and you feel like a fool thinking it would have gone any differently. Do not let yourself get stuck in their misery!

People will get angry because you are cutting ties with them, but that's to be expected. They are not used to having these boundaries with you and they can't understand why this is happening all of a sudden. It will probably be hard saying goodbye to some of your friends or family. Just do what you have to do to continue your growth. You don't have to make a big spectacle of cutting your ties. Just let them know that you are taking time to be alone and work on yourself. Don't blame anyone for anything. Just ask them to honor your alone time, and I'm sure they probably will. Some of them may try to text you the next day or come over to your house to gossip. Reinforce what you asked them to do. Let them know that gossiping is not helping your growth. Tell them that you need to be alone and you do not want to text. Or just turn your phone off if you are able to. It may take time to get the point across to them, but eventually they should ease off.

Your friends might try to bring up conversation about your ex just to let you know what he's doing. This is not good for you! I know it seems juicy and you want to know where he is and who he is with, but this will do nothing but hurt you more than you already do. You can't heal if you keep opening up that old wound. It's like picking your scab off – your body is trying to heal itself but you keep picking at it and then it takes ten times longer to heal. Then, when it finally heals, it's scarred. Don't do this to yourself. If your friends try to bring up your ex in conversation, just redirect them and be firm. Don't be afraid to stand up for yourself.

I'm sure many of your loved ones will want to give you advice on your relationship issues (if they haven't already). They mean well. Just nod and listen to what they are saying with an open heart. Just because they give you advice doesn't mean you have to take it. But we should always try to honor the advice our loved ones give us. Their intentions are usually good. They will probably ask you why you broke up. You don't have to engage in this. Just come up with a short and to-the-point answer to tell everyone in this circumstance. If you keep saying that answer, people will eventually get bored and stop asking. They will understand that they aren't going to get any more information from you.

Creating a healthy environment is not just about your peaceful space at home, it's about the people you surround yourself with. Be aware of the company you keep. If you can't find anyone who looks like they would be uplifting, then be by yourself. No company is better than bad company. Eventually you will really learn to enjoy your time alone. It's nice getting to do whatever you want whenever you want without anyone saying otherwise. Make sure your sacred space is a place that makes you the happiest. This is a delicate time for you. You need the proper environment to help you grow. It may be difficult if you live in a crowded house, if you are a single mother, or if you live in a big city. Maybe you could leave for work a little bit early and go park by the water somewhere. Maybe your quiet time could be early in the morning before the kids wake up or late at night when they go to sleep. Do what you need to do to make a space for yourself. Even if it's making a blanket fort in your closet. If you have a relaxing space to be, you will feel so much better. Take the time to make it everything you want it to be. Work on your vision boards and do things that make your soul happy. Surround yourself with beautiful pictures, quotes, smells, etc. These are the things that will ignite your soul.

Chapter 7: I Don't Know Why I'm Like This

"Hurt people hurt people."

— Pastor Rick Warren

If you have air in your lungs and blood in your veins, then you have probably experienced some type of hardship in your life. The world can be a very cruel place with angry people. Some of you have probably had more than one horrible thing happen in your life. I'm sorry you have to go through painful experiences that don't make any sense. The only reason why someone hurt you in the first place is because they are hurting inside too. They are looking for any way to get that pain out of them and into someone or something else. They will do whatever it takes to get rid of it, but of course, it never works by inflicting it on others. It only deepens the wound.

It's hard, but I want you to think about the things that have happened to you in the past that really hurt you. Think about how you were feeling at the time. What were you thinking when it happened? How old were you? What did you try to do to make it better? Did this instance make you become a different person? Probably, this painful moment triggered a new habit in you or a new thought process. It's only natural. Our minds want to try and create a defense mechanism from that pain we felt. This builds up walls between us and the world around. Don't beat yourself up for being a certain way because of a trauma that has happened to you in the past. Just know that it's what you needed at the time to survive. But now, that time is over. It can't hurt you anymore unless you let it. It's time to understand your defense mechanisms and move on from them.

Do you build up walls every time someone tries to know you on a deeper level? Do you use comedy to detour from feeling painful emotions? Are you stuck in a childish mindset, acting like a baby because you were coddled during your traumatic time? Make a list of the hardships you have faced in your lifetime. Think about how those instances triggered ways of thinking, how you act, how you speak, how you think, how you deal with other people, etc. Think of any negative outcome that may have been caused from this painful period of your life. The only way we can understand why we are the way we are is if we get really clear on what caused it and how we can move forward.

For me, my biggest heartbreak was my parents getting divorced when I was ten. I remember them fighting a lot but I was not expecting them to separate. I cried so hard when they sat me and my sister down to tell us. They made sure to let us know it was not our fault. As time went on, I remember having this persistent thought in the back of my head. It would say "Why am I not good enough for him to stay?" I couldn't figure it out. I remember putting on my brave face when he moved out and trying to be strong. I only cried about him one time after he left. Something in me changed and from that time in my life forward, I acted like I didn't need a dad. I convinced myself that I was completely fine. As I got older, I started seeking that love from the guys who would give me attention. It started with my first serious relationship and continued on throughout my twenties. When I finally sat down to be alone in 2016 it all made sense. I was seeking the love and approval from guys because I had not dealt with my daddy issues. I was seeking my worth in these guys because I didn't feel worthy enough for my own father to stay. Then I understood that I had to find my own self-worth. Either way, it was just a divorce, it had nothing to do with whether or not I was good enough to keep my dad around. I had made this deep-seated childhood issue follow me through my life from that point forward because I couldn't deal with it at the time. I could have saved myself from so much heartbreak if I would have just taken time to heal properly.

Do you self-sabotage? That's such a frustrating thing to witness. I've seen many clients at the place I work who will do so well in the program and then a few days before they are scheduled to discharge, you can see them falling back into their same old habits. Then they show up a few weeks later, relapsed. It's okay that they came back. We are always glad they come back instead of continuing to spiral out of control. It's just sad to see them in these self-destructive behaviors. We can do all we can to try and teach them the steps to get through it, but sometimes it takes a few relapses to finally sink in. Think about what you do to self-sabotage. Do you find a way to throw a wrench in it when things are going too well? James used to do this. We could be having a great day together with no fights, then he would say something mean or make a comment to upset me and that would start a fight. I couldn't figure out why he was like this. It's important that you figure out where that comes from. Most of the time it's because of something that happened to you when you were little. I don't think people are really born this way. I believe it is acquired over time. Either way, it's your responsibility to find out why and to resolve this issue for good.

So, what are your issues? Do you have daddy issues as well? Did you have trouble being intimate with your husband because you were raped? Did that make you have trust issues? Do you see all men as trash because you never had a respectful man around you in your whole life? Do you feel like you are going to be left because that's all you ever knew from any man who came around in your childhood? Do you feel like you have to be perfect all the time for your man because that's how your mother acted? Get honest with yourself. Get down in the dirt and dig up those deep roots. The only way to get rid of it is to dig deep enough and tear it up. This might be another one of those days that you ugly cry and feel like you are back to square one. I promise, you are doing great. Work through the pain you are feeling and remember to write down your thought process. Learn from this pain, don't just wallow in it. See the walls you have built up over time and what caused them. Be kind and honor the broken parts of yourself.

I know it probably feels horrible right now, but you are doing wonderfully. Repeat these words: "The wound is the place where the Light enters you." That quote is from an ancient poet named Rumi. I think it's such a beautiful way to see your pain. Don't just lay down and accept your pain as nothing but pain. Take a stand and see your pain as potential. It's potential for you to grow and experience happiness and healing. Some say that a broken heart is the only way for more love to get in. I know that trying to see these painful experiences in a positive light may seem almost insulting, but I am not trying to be insensitive. I'm only trying to use your pain for your benefit. Not only can it benefit you, but your pain can be used to benefit those around you if you choose to grow from it. You can become a beacon of light for others who are going through the same situations you went through. When they see you they can say "Well, if she made it through, then so can I." What power you have! And as you help them heal, it will only make you become stronger. Try to see these traumatic experiences in a new light. It might take you a very long time, and that's okay. Just keep making an effort to rise above.

Some of you may move on from this lesson fairly quickly, but for others it may take you quite a while. Take however much time you need to truly process through it. Even if it's a year or more – don't be ashamed. Remember, you are trying to get this done right the first time so you can live the life you are intended to live. It's not about how fast you can overcome it, it's about being genuinely past this pain. Process it as much as you can and if you need to take a week off, then do it. Just don't set it aside and act like it will go away. It will find its way to the surface again, I promise. It will get easier with time though. You might need to write a nasty letter to the person who hurt you and then burn it. Or maybe you need to take a boxing class with that person's face taped to the punching bag. You could even envision yourself in front of that person and see them for who they really are: someone who is hurting. You could see them, and you could say "I forgive you." Make your peace with it and continue with your life. However you need to get through it, it doesn't matter. As long as it is healthy for you, and you aren't hurting yourself or others.

This step is tough. It's nitty-gritty and maybe even annoying. That's fine, as long as you complete this step. Don't sweep this one under the rug because it's too hard to deal with. Don't make excuses because you don't want to feel these emotions. We are done with excuses at this point. You are already in this healing process too deep to turn around now. Might as well do what's necessary to keep moving forward. You are strong and completely capable of handling your issues. Don't think of yourself as anything less than a warrior. Remember that you are the only one who can give yourself the life you desire, the life you were meant to live. Do not give up on yourself just because things get tough. Spend time in your thoughts and really conjure up what has been the root of your problems for all these years. Notice it for what it is and create a list of ways to change it. Change it in every aspect so that it has no power over you anymore. It's time for you to take back your power and make this life what you want it to be, not what was dealt upon you.

Chapter 8: My Thoughts Are Out of Control

"A man cannot be comfortable without his own approval."

— Mark Twain

What do you think about yourself on a daily basis? How do you see yourself every day? Most likely, it's in a negative light. Society puts so much pressure on us to live up to certain expectations, so it's only natural that we subconsciously begin to feel not good enough. Do you think you are too fat, too stupid, too weird, too clingy, too annoying? We are our own biggest critics. Probably none of those things are true about you. We get frustrated with ourselves because we can't seem to change, but how do we expect to change when we don't first change the thoughts from within?

Everything starts from the mind. If you want to achieve something in your life, you need to begin by imagining yourself having that thing. Focus on it with all your power and summon it up often. We can't expect to attract good things and to be successful if we are constantly thinking bad thoughts about ourselves or the situation. My mom always used to tell me when I was little, "If you change the way you look at things, the things you look at change." This is a quote from Dr. Wayne Dyer. It means if you keep looking at your situation in a negative way, it will stay a negative situation. If you start seeing the situation positively then the situation will begin to become a positive one. It's so true! Not everything we do in life is fun or something we see as a good situation. Maybe you have a job you hate or a roommate that is really mean. The only way we can do something about it is either quit, move out, or just change your perspective about it. Most likely, you need that job right now, or you aren't done with your lease with your roommate. Your back may be up against a wall at this point. When our circumstances get to this point, it becomes even more frustrating. Not only do you hate the situation you're in, but you are stuck in it for God only knows how long and that makes you feel depressed or angry. You must get control over your thoughts to make it through.

Start finding positive things about the job you do. Maybe it's one customer that brings you happiness every day. You can focus on making them happy so they continue to come see you every day. Or maybe it's taking the trash out in the morning before your shop opens. It gets you away from everyone else for a moment of peace. Relish that moment and remember how you feel. You can bring up those feelings of peace any time you wish, especially when you start getting stressed out or upset. Perhaps your roommate is really mean to you for no reason. Try to understand where she is coming from or what her situation is. Maybe try connecting with her on something small. That will begin a conversation that can open the door for deeper conversations in the future. Find something every day that will connect you two and eventually, she should warm up to you. Then the tension will be gone or maybe you can talk about finding balance with each other. Even if getting to know her doesn't work and she just stays mean, find something that brings you peace in the house every day and focus on that. Remember that feeling so that you can summon it up whenever you feel sad or frustrated with your situation.

Keep practicing these tactics of rewiring your thoughts. Find the good things in every instance and it will start to become easier. When I was in high school, I ran over a nail with my car and popped the tire. It was beyond patching. I had to buy a whole new tire. I remember someone talking about how that was so annoying and how I must be angry it happened. I said "No, I'm glad it happened to me instead of someone who can't afford it right now." I would rather my tire have popped than a single mother struggling to buy groceries. When you try to find the positive things in life, it becomes easier to see so many reasons to be happy.

My whole life I've had a problem with staying positive in how I saw my relationships with men. Whenever I would get into a new relationship with a guy, something in me would bring up this sense of doom in my spirit. It's like I expected the relationship to end in a bad way, even if things were going perfect. I would start dating a new guy, we would be so happy, but in the back of my mind I could envision the end being messy and heartbreaking. Why was that? I truly believe it's because I grew up with my parents being divorced. As I've mentioned, when I was ten years old my dad left. That's probably what set the tone for my future relationships. As time went on, the more breakups I had, it just added fuel to that fire. I couldn't see any guy being faithful and staying. It seemed like an impossible feat. It's a sad feeling when you enter a relationship expecting heartbreak. Do you ever catch yourself thinking these thoughts? Do you expect to be cheated on because it always seems to happen? Do you expect him to lose interest or to not treat you as good anymore because it's what always happens? How can our relationships thrive if this is the expectation we set?

Yes, these things may have happened in the past, multiple times, but it doesn't mean this is the way it will be forever. Obviously, you are doing what it takes to become a different woman now. If you take your growth seriously and move on from this then your relationships will never be the same. You won't have to go into a new love with expectation of heartbreak. You won't ever have to go into a relationship with the end in mind. Now you will be able to know that it will be as successful as you both make it. Just because you have been cheated on or treated badly in the past does not mean that is your life sentence. Your life is meant to be beautiful and happy. It's time to do the work on ourselves so that we can experience the life we are meant to live.

I watched a video from Iyanla Vanzant teaching in Oprah's life class called "get unstuck from your story" and it was very motivational. She spoke about how we need to tell the absolute truth about who we are, what we want, and what we are willing and not willing to do to get there. She said we need to acknowledge what we did to contribute to our pain, but don't get stuck there. She talked about how once you are able to have a vision for your life, that is what will pull you through. It's such a great video because it's so straightforward and simple. We have to see what we do that contributes to our pain so that we can stop those self-sabotaging behaviors. Once we see that, we can stop ourselves from doing them in the future. Then, we can envision the way we want ourselves and our lives to be and we can make the conscious effort to strive toward our goals. On the days you feel sad or angry or frustrated with your situation, the vision will pull you forward.

Another incredible video from one of Oprah's life classes was from Bishop T.D. Jakes. In the video he dropped a bomb on everyone, including Oprah. He said "By holding onto your history, you do it at the expense of your destiny." He went on to explain how you are a limited resource. If you spend all your energy focusing and obsessing about what has happened to you in the past, you have no energy to give toward focusing on your future and becoming the person you desire to be. We cannot be pulled in all these different directions. Your life will go in the way in which you focus on. Look at your surroundings and you will see where your focus has been. I highly suggest you watch these videos and watch more of their content. Iyanla and Bishop Jakes both have so many inspirational videos and books. They helped me through my hard times and I believe they can help you through yours as well.

Who do you find inspirational? Make a list of the people you look up to and what traits you love about them. When you make this list, do you notice people who are known for being positive in the world or do you notice you have more people who are known for being the bad-boy type, or maybe they are known for more bad things than good. Take notice of what type of list you have. It's important for us to look up to people who will be a good example. Find the positive aspects you love about these people and strive to have those qualities for yourself. We don't need to try to copy these people and become something we are not, but we should always be reaching to become better in our own selves. Don't try to be *someone* different, just try to be different from the way you have been.

How do you speak about yourself? Whether it be inner or outer dialogue. Do you always speak about yourself in a negative way? Do you say things like "Oh, stupid me, I forgot" or "Look at my muffin tops. I'm disgusting!" If people hear you speaking about yourself like this then that gives them permission to speak of you negatively as well. You set the tone for what you expect. When you speak about yourself badly then you are opening the door for others to do it as well. Not only that, people get tired of trying to always console you. At first, they will say "No, you look great!" or "Quit beating yourself up all the time" but as time goes on, they will eventually stop trying to change your mind for you. They have their own problems to deal with and it gets tiring to try to fix your self-image as well. Or maybe you are the opposite. Maybe your self-image on the inside is negative but you speak about yourself as if you are the hottest person on the planet. If your inner dialogue doesn't match the outer dialogue, then it's pointless. You will still be stressed out and insecure. Not only that, people get tired of hearing how high and mighty you think you are. Being egotistical is not an endearing quality. You might be saying, "No, I have plenty of friends who love it when I pump myself up" but most likely they speak this way about themselves also, being just as insecure on the inside. Just as we discussed in a previous chapter – your vibe attracts your tribe. Everyone is pumping themselves up on the outside but deep down they are all crying. The ones who are humble are the ones who have balance within.

Think about what you attract when you speak negatively about yourself. If a manipulative man overhears you speaking negatively of yourself, then you automatically become an easy target for him. If you have something he wants *and* you have low self-esteem, you will be easy to prey on. Can you think of any exes that have done this to you? Or have you ever said "I'm always broke. I never have money" or "I always get the worst job at work." If you continue to expect the worst and speak it into existence, then it will continue to happen. Try turning your words into positive ones and see how your life changes. It may not be an immediate turn-around, but after some time you will be able to see positive changes in your life. What you say is what you get.

Think about what you really want in a relationship. Do you want love, respect, positive affirmation, understanding? If you want these types of qualities, then you have to become these qualities. If you want love then you need to be loving, be willing to be loved, and love yourself first. If you want respect, then you need to be respectful and you need to respect yourself first. You get the picture. You can't demand these things from other people if you aren't willing to give them to yourself first and you aren't willing to give them to others. There's nothing more infuriating than having a boss who demands respect from you but does not offer it in return. Doesn't it make you want to give them the finger and quit? This is the same thing in every relationship in your life. My main point here is that if you want love then you have to give it to yourself first. If you want respect, then you must respect yourself. People will only do what you let them do. You set the bar for what you expect.

Rewiring your thoughts not only happens with what you say and think about yourself, but it also has to do with who and what you surround yourself with. If you are constantly watching shows that have nothing but drama, cheating, getting lit, being disgusting and immoral, then how do you expect to become more than that? How do you expect to rise above your current situation if you surround yourself with people who are always negative, who speak badly of others, who only want to get trashed with you? You can't heal in an environment like that. Watching shows that normalize cheating is not going to help you to expect more than that. Rewiring your thoughts is more than just what you think – it's everything that surrounds you as well. This goes back to creating a healthy environment for yourself to grow in. You can do so much work and start to become the beautiful person you were meant to be, but once you get around these same negative people or watch the same old junky shows on TV, I guarantee you will start to slip back into that old mindset. Your brain will automatically want to go with what is easy and familiar. Protect your growth as if it's the most delicate thing on this earth. Protect it like it's your baby and don't let anyone around it that could harm it. This time in your life is so important, so please don't derail what you've learned just because your old friends miss partying with you.

I urge you to really pay attention to your thoughts in the coming weeks. Take notice of them and when you see a bad one, reword it immediately. Don't even let one negative thought slip by. It's going to seem hard for a little bit, but it will get better with time. Look up to positive people and strive toward the aspects you love about them. Speak kindly of yourself, always. Expect greatness from this point forward. The days of being cheated on, being treated badly, being taken advantage of, those are all over now as long as you choose for them to be. If you are truly ready to move on, then your life will never be the same. Give yourself a hug for continuing this journey. Your stem is getting stronger and you are growing more into what you were intended to be. Keep going! Be proud of yourself.

Chapter 9: How Do I Find Love Again?

"We must be our own before we can be another's."

— Ralph Waldo Emerson

I love this concept. It seems so simple, and yet not many do it. I know many of you are probably thinking, "Yeah that seems great and wonderful, but I am *lonely*!" I understand. It's okay to be lonely sometimes. It's going to happen. That feeling won't stay forever if you continue to follow the steps in this book. Loneliness is going to happen, but it will only be temporary if you continue to grow from your pain, spend time with yourself, understand yourself, and do what it takes to be strong on your own. If you are happy with yourself and your company, can you ever really be lonely?

The majority of the people on earth are looking for love in all the wrong places. They look online for people to puff up their ego with nice comments. They find another man to date so they can feel like they are worthy of love. They look for approval of their parents that they will probably never get, they try to find love by sacrificing their entire self to another person only to get nothing but betrayal in the end. It's a sad sight. I can't even count how many girls I see on my Facebook who post almost daily about how much they love their partner. They ooze on and on about him and then a few months or a few years go by and she's ranting on Facebook about what a scumbag he is for cheating on her. She sacrifices so much for him, putting her friends on hold, paying for everything, hyping him up to be something he's not, and it still ends so horribly.

Have you done this before? I'm sure many of you have. I have, many times. It always ends badly. For this chapter I want you to make a list of all the wonderful qualities you brought to the table in your past relationships. I know you probably had a lot to offer these guys, so take some time and create your list. Once you've done this, I want you to take a look at how big it probably is. For some reason, we women feel like we have to take care of everything all the time. We feel like we have to always look good, smell good, act how he likes, make his favorite foods, pay all the bills, do what he likes in bed, take care of his dogs, whatever. If we aren't constantly being perfect at everything all the time, we start to feel a lot of anxiety that he will leave us. If we aren't acting just right then he will get upset and that will snowball into the reason why he will cheat or leave you. What a horrible way to live! I have been in that mindset for almost the entirety of my 20s. No wonder why we are always so stressed out and snippy. We are only human. Now look at your list again. Imagine how great your life would be if you did those things for yourself. Imagine how your life would change when you put the power back into your own hands instead of someone else's. You would not need to seek these things from anyone else because you would already be giving them to yourself. What a concept.

So here's my golden egg of a lesson for this chapter: the love you seek is already within, and only you can give it to yourself. The reason why our relationships never live up to our expectations is because we are expecting that other person to give us everything that only we can give ourselves. No matter how good that relationship may be, it just isn't quite right, is it? There's something that feels "off" and you can't put your finger on it. It's because you are expecting them to give you only what you can give yourself. I believe in God. I'm not here to push any religion or views on you, but in my opinion, I strongly believe that God equipped us with everything we ever need to be happy. It is already in us – we just have to dig deep and pull it out. The reason why you may have had fights or tension in your marriage was because you were expecting them to give you everything that they would never be able to give. Don't get me wrong, I'm not saying everything is your fault. It takes two to tango. I'm just saying that most people are always looking for this love in other people, and they will forever be disappointed if they continue this route. Stop putting this expectation on others! It's not fair for you to do to them and it's not fair for them to do to you. How is anyone expected to live up to those standards? They can't. You can't. So this is my resolution: Become the love you seek so desperately.

I believe self-love is the primary source of our happiness and fulfillment. It's hard to go by in life if you don't even like yourself, let alone love yourself. How can you expect anyone else to really love you if you don't even love yourself? Just like we discussed in a previous chapter, you set the standard for how others treat you. If you can't love yourself then how do you expect anything more from another person? Take time to look at yourself for exactly what you are. Get really honest about the person you are and the person you have been. If you are not happy with it, figure out some ways to rise above it. Change your habits. Change your thoughts. Take however long you need to become the woman you desire to be. What would make you happy? What can you do to make the world a better place? One way to make the world a better place is to first make yourself better. Get to know yourself better than anyone knows you. Spend time thinking about your thought process, what makes you tick, what makes you excited, what are your breaking points? Understand exactly who you are. That way, when the right one comes along, they will be able to understand you too. You will expect nothing less than what you set as your standards.

During this time, make sure you figure out what your boundaries are. I know many of you have probably thrown your boundaries out the window just to make your man happy at the time. I did that many times in my past and it was such a painful part of my life. I was dying on the inside, but I told him it was okay because I didn't want him to leave me. Love makes us do crazy things. Take some time to remember what your boundaries are or make new ones if needed. Boundaries are healthy and necessary. They show that not only do you respect yourself, but you expect to be respected. Stand up for yourself and what you believe in. It's time to regrow your backbone.

Self-love seems cliché and dreamy but it's completely attainable. You just have to practice it. Don't think "I'll love myself when I'm not so fat" or "I'll love myself when I get this all figured out." No, you need to love yourself right now in this moment, just as you are. There's no better time than right now. You are beautiful and perfect in this moment of transformation. Take a hard look at yourself and how much you are trying. Can you feel any change yet? If so, think about how exciting that is! Look how much you've done already. If you can't see any change yet, don't stress out. Trust that it's part of your unique process and love yourself through it. This is all coming together in perfect, divine timing. You are doing exactly what you need right now. Be easy on yourself.

Imagine if people treated you so good all the time. Everyone was kind, helpful, loving, and respectful of you. How would that make you feel? Well, this can be a goal you have for yourself. You have to understand that the way people treat you is simply a reflection on how you see yourself. If your ex ever treated you badly when you were together it's because you would not treat yourself good. Maybe he didn't show you any respect. It's probably because you didn't have respect for yourself and you didn't have healthy boundaries with him. Did he speak about you in a negative way? He probably saw you doing it to yourself and he knew it was okay. The way people treat us is just a reflection of the way we treat ourselves. When we begin to speak kindly to ourselves then it makes us become happier and it changes our whole demeanor. Not only will you speak kindly to yourself, but it will be contagious, and you will most likely start speaking sweetly to others as well. People will start speaking kindly to you also. If you respect yourself, people will feel that and treat you with respect also. Think of how you want to be treated and start taking the steps needed to be that way to yourself.

I hope that one day, when you have taken time and healed yourself properly, you will find the person meant for you. I hope that you will instantly feel that connection with that person and be able to spend the rest of your lives together in happiness. If you do find this person, understand that you will not need external love and validation from them, because you will already have everything you need within you. You will have all the love you ever need inside, and when they come along, they can bask in that love with you. Neither of you will expect anything but company from each other. It will be happy, sweet, respectful, and anxiety-free. If this seems like a long shot to you, please take extra time to imagine yourself in this scenario until you start to believe it is an option for you. Maybe you don't ever want to be in a relationship again. That's completely fine. I just want you to understand that you will be okay no matter what, whether in a relationship or not.

After I had spent the year alone in 2016 I felt like a totally different person. I found a happiness that I had never experienced. I felt joyful, peaceful, and completely content being alone. I had all the love I could ask for. I knew I was going to be okay from that point forward. Around the end of the year I sat down in my room one night and made a list of thirty qualities I wanted in my life partner. I pinned it up in my closet along with some other motivational quotes. Every day I would glance at that list as I went to get dressed for the day. One night in November I was saying my prayers for the night and I asked God to bring me the one I was meant to marry. I told him I felt good on my own, but I was ready to have a partner for life. About a month later, at the beginning of December I had a girlfriend at work who randomly told me about her friend who was single. His name was Chris and she said he was a wonderful guy, and really cute. She showed me pictures of him and tried to get me to go on a date with him. I turned her down and said, "I'm not sure if I'm ready just yet." I was completely contradicting my prayers. She left me alone about it for a while. Then at the beginning of January 2017 she brought it up again. I agreed that I would talk to him online so I could see how he was. We started talking through Facebook messenger and we seemed to hit it off pretty well. One night I was invited over to my friend's house for a bonfire and Chris was there. I wasn't expecting to meet him that night. It was just me, Chris, our mutual friend and her boyfriend. They left us alone for a while so we could talk more. Chris and I ended up talking for hours into the night. It felt like we had known each other forever. It was fairly cold that night but we sat on the boat ramp with our feet dangling in the freezing water. We had a very strong connection and I was so happy to get to know him. He continued to pursue me and I was very hesitant. I didn't want to make the wrong decision and I was nervous about relationships because of my track record. I decided to trust myself and how far I had come. We started dating and never looked back. He's been an incredible partner and I know I've found the one I was meant to be with. It turns out, Chris was praying to meet the right one at the same time I was. We had both gone through heartbreak and cheaters, but we came out stronger and it brought us together at the perfect time. I believe we do well together because we don't look for the love from the other person. We have our love within and we both enjoy it together. We each contribute to the relationship and lift each other up. It feels like we have been together for twenty very happy years. This is the type of love I hope you find. It's a great feeling when you don't throw all your expectations onto the other person. Both of you can be relaxed and content which makes for a healthier relationship. Find your love within first. That's the only way you can truly find this peace in your relationships. It may take you're a year or more, but it is worth it in the grand scheme of things. If you get it right this time, then you will be set for life. Don't skimp on your growth process. Do the work and I promise you will have such a happier life.

"If you want to see the beloveds face, polish the mirror, gaze into that space."

—Rumi

"In any relationship in which two people become one, the end result is two half people."

— Wayne W. Dyer

"The minute I heard my first love story,
I started looking for you, not knowing
how blind that was.
Lovers don't finally meet somewhere.
They're in each other all along."

— Rumi

Chapter 10: Now What?

So, do you feel any different yet? Some of you probably can tell the difference in how you feel and how you act compared to when you started. It depends on how slowly you worked through this book. For others, maybe you still feel stuck. It's okay if you do. Sometimes it will just take a while for you to feel the difference. Each person is unique. Please don't confine yourself to a timeline to get this done. Remember, you are getting it done right, not getting it done fast. Take all the time you need and be patient with yourself. Love yourself through the process. Your healing is a top priority right now.

Even if you are feeling wonderful, like a whole new woman, it's important that you keep practicing. You may feel like you have it all together and nothing can stop you. I guarantee there will be times where you might slip back into your old ways of thinking for a day or so. Don't beat yourself up on these days. Just try again tomorrow. Making yourself feel bad about having an off day is completely counter-productive. Maybe you might see a guy who reminds you of an ex that ignites that old fire in you. Be aware of your thought process! Make sure what you are thinking is moving you forward and not pulling you back to the familiar. Honor the work you've done by not falling back into your old habits. You may want to connect with your old friends or family members at some point. That's fine – just make sure you feel strong enough in yourself before you do. They may want to go back to how things were before you took your time of solitude. Will that be beneficial to you? They may want to go to the club with you or sit around and talk trash about people again. They will most likely expect to be hanging out with the same person they used to. When they see how different you are, they will probably bring it up and possibly make you feel bad about how you are now. Think about these scenarios. Will they serve the greater good for you? If not, then you might need to limit your time with these people. Most likely, they are used to not having you around much right now. You can slowly introduce yourself back into the social circle without plunging head first. If you feel yourself being influenced in a negative way, then work your way back out again. Please, don't sacrifice your new self just to appease these past relationships. Your success and happiness are far more important.

Please, don't ever stay stagnant with your growth process. Always try to find some way to grow as a person on a daily basis. Whether it be watching videos online about a new way to do something or learning a new skill, taking a college course you find interesting, trying to understand someone who seems really difficult, reading books, whatever. Try to find something new every day that you can grow from. Once we stay still, we have the potential of getting stuck there. You are such an incredible person and you've been blessed with a brain that functions properly. Might as well take advantage of what you've been given. When we stay stagnant, that's when anxiety and depression can creep back in and wreak havoc on our mentality. When you aren't learning a new skill, find a way to grow spiritually every day. Take time to meditate. Imagine yourself in a new place. Maybe you could see yourself floating in space surrounded by stars, or deep under the ocean swimming with sea creatures. Expand your mind and try new practices. Do that one thing that brings your heart joy. Paint, dance, sing, garden, build things, redecorate, hike, do whatever it is that makes your spirit light up. This helps keep the focus on you and your mental health. When you start to fall back into your old mindset, you probably are only thinking of the negative aspects of yourself and those around you. Life begins to look bleak again. Don't let yourself get in this position. Keep growing. Stay thirsty for the wonderful things life has to offer and be willing to offer life more as well. Remember your vision of the woman you want to become. Are you there yet? If not, find ways to make it to her and work on it daily. If you are tired of growing, take a day or two off. Reflect on how far you've come. Just sit back and enjoy the view from how far you have climbed. Take a few days to relax and then go at it again strong after some rest.

I'm the type of person who is almost obsessive with self-growth. I have probably a hundred e-mails in my inbox daily that are from self-help gurus, business gurus, meditation guides, numerology forecasts, daily bible verses to reflect on, those types of things. I try to read all of them every day and get what I can from them. I find myself getting extremely overwhelmed a lot of the time though. It's almost getting to be too much. I love finding a new way to grow every day but when people bombard you with this many e-mails it's like information overload. Sometimes I think to myself: *Am I really learning?* It's hard to learn one thing properly if you're trying to shove 15 different life lessons in your brain on the daily. If this is how you are feeling, then take a step back from it and give yourself a break. It's perfectly fine to take a little time off from self-improvement and move into a state of self-reflection. Just don't stay there too long.

Remember, sometimes you might have to go through this book a few times to really let it sink in and learn from it. Many of us don't learn a lesson just once. It usually takes a few times of learning to really stick with us. We are only human. Or maybe you feel like you've really got Chapters 3 to 6 down perfectly but you're having trouble with Chapter 7. Revisit whatever chapters you need whenever you need them. This is your tool to have on hand whenever you start feeling bad or get confused. You might even find a new person to date and go through another bad breakup to finally get it in your mind well enough. I hope it doesn't come down to that. Whatever happens, just know that you are doing the best you can with what you know. We always have and we always will. It's not like people wake up in the morning and say "Hm, I really feel like failing at life today." No. People don't go into things with hopes to fail or get hurt. We almost always do our best and have good intentions. Don't beat yourself up if you don't get it right the first time. Praise yourself for the good things you do. Expect to do well. I'm going to use the universal baby steps example now. When a baby is taking her first steps and falls, people praise her for the one or two steps she took. They don't spank her for falling. The praise makes her do better. She doesn't get frustrated at the fact that she fell, she just keeps trying despite what happens. Eventually she gets stronger and can walk with no issue. Every once and a while she might trip and fall again, but it's to be expected. We are the same way. Even when you feel so strong, years from now, and you may be in a really great relationship, you might have a bad day that reminds you of where you came from. That's okay. You are strong, but it doesn't mean you are invincible. Just keep praising yourself for the good ways you are improving and don't beat yourself up for the bad days. Keep growing forward.

If you do find the right one after time, don't stop implementing these steps. You may have reached a goal of finding a healthy relationship, but you need to always keep yourself healthy first. Keep loving yourself properly. Keep giving yourself what you need. Take time to be alone so you can spend time with yourself. Keep journaling and doing the things that bring you joy. Keep speaking positively about yourself and have confidence. Keep finding the things you need inward instead of through them. If something happens that upsets you, reflect on what is causing the hurt and try to figure out what caused this reaction. Work through that hurt and learn from it so it will not continue to have control over you. Don't stop visiting your place of solitude just because you found someone new. You are the most important relationship in your life. If you don't continue to keep a healthy relationship with yourself, then your other relationships will not make it. Continue your self-improvement and don't let anyone ever stop you. When the right one comes along, they will love it and honor it.

Your growth process will never be done. Please, don't get frustrated because you feel like you should be done with it by now. Self-improvement is like laundry: You will never truly be done. If you are, it's either because you are stuck or you are dead. For a long time I would get so angry at myself because I felt like I should be farther along than I was. I look around at my friends who are younger than me who are married with beautiful houses and going on their second child. They take vacations and it looks like their marriages are so happy. They have it all together. I would start to compare myself to them and that would bring so much sadness into my life. I felt like a failure. I was nowhere near having what they had. It made me feel so ashamed of myself. Over time I had to teach myself not to compare my story with people around me. People are very good at making their lives look wonderful online. In actuality they may be having all sorts of huge problems that nobody knows about. Just because they have the things I want doesn't mean they are smarter or more mature than me. I may know more about life than they do. They may know more about taxes than I do. Everyone knows different things, it doesn't make one person smarter or more successful than the other. Comparison is such a crippling feeling. Please, do yourself a favor if you are like I used to be. Stop making yourself feel like a failure just because you don't have what someone else has. The best thing you can do is to look at someone you admire and just strive to have the qualities they possess. Don't sit there and wish you were that person. Obviously, that's never going to happen. Take the aspects you love from that person and work toward achieving that. You will eliminate the shame from comparison and replace it with achievable goals. Even though they look like they have life figured out, they are still just learning and growing like me and you. We are all in the same boat.

Be proud of yourself for where you are right now. Whether you feel like a totally new person, or if you feel like you've barely grown at all. Love yourself in this moment just as you are. Know that your process is exactly how it needs to be and you are trying your best. Keep a positive mindset so that you can stay above any troubled waters. Take your time and go through these chapters as many times as you need for it to finally stick. And if you feel like you are finally over your breakups and your heartbreaks, don't forget what you have learned in this book. Continue to practice these steps whenever you can so that you stay strong in yourself. I'm proud of you and I'm so excited for you to have the life you have been craving. You truly deserve greatness.

Chapter 11: It All Makes Sense Now!

"It all makes sense now!" If you are like me, that's exactly what you are thinking or have been thinking for a while. It's interesting how we can't see what the issue is when the bad stuff is happening. We are looking around at what the situation looked like and what went wrong in our relationship with this person, but we don't really think to look inward. We blame the external factors: "she must have been prettier than me," "she must have been easy," "I probably made him mad that night which is why he left me," "I say stupid things that make him mad," "I ask too much from him." Have you caught yourself saying or thinking those things in the past? Have you almost always blamed yourself for why he treated you the way he did or why he cheated on you? I bet you see things so much clearer now. Our problem was that we were not looking within.

We didn't think to look at ourselves. We didn't think that by speaking badly of ourselves and not giving ourselves the respect we needed was causing a chain reaction for others to be this way toward us. It all makes sense now. How did we ever expect to be treated properly if we never set healthy boundaries? Of course he would do whatever he wanted – you never opposed. You never drew the line and said: "That is not okay with me." If we would have made boundaries then he would have either left or been respectful of you. How did we ever expect to get a kind and loving relationship if we never were kind and loving to ourselves? How did we ever expect someone else to treat us a certain way if we couldn't even treat ourselves that way? Man, it really can make you feel like an idiot in hindsight. But we don't feel that way, do we? No. We are confident and proud of ourselves for being brought to this new revelation. Now we see what we were missing: ourselves. Understanding the lessons in this book is like a key to the door that will lead you into that life you have been wanting for so long. These lessons not only help you with breakups, but they can help in so many areas of your lives.

If you are having trouble in any area of your life, try to implement these steps to move forward. Maybe it's with your job, your children, your spouse, or anything else you may need help with. You can work through the pain after you take time to understand it. You can implement positive thinking and take time in your sacred space to reflect on the issue. You can try to see what is going on inward that is causing this to happen outward. All the steps may not apply to your issue, but I'm sure one or two of these chapters would help guide you through.

The time for suffering is over. It's your time to heal and grow and become the most beautiful soul that you were created to be. Once you've healed from this and moved on, you can begin to heal any past relationships with friends or family that have been damaged. You can begin to form new, healthy relationships with these people and instill boundaries that are respectful to both of you. You can not only heal these relationships, but ensure that they will not be damaged again by the men you choose to love. What a wonderful feeling to know you will not hurt your loved ones again.

When James and I broke up, I felt like my relationship with my family was so damaged it would never be the same. I felt so much shame about the fact that I had put them through that. I should have believed my family over him, because they have always been here for me and wanted what was best. I did my time healing myself and spent plenty of time alone. I made my apologies to my family and they forgave me just as they always do. I still wasn't sure if things would ever feel the same as before, but I tried to become trustworthy again. As time went on, things became better and we were back to normal as a family. I continue to work on myself. I made a vow to myself that I would never let a man come between me and my family again. They have always been supportive and they have loved me despite my best efforts. I made them deal with horrible exes. I have ditched them so I could go be with who I was dating at the time. That is time and memories that I will never get back. I will never let it happen again. I have been blessed with a great family who never gave up on me. Do you have any family members or friends who are like this? Don't give up on them either. Work on yourself and become better so that you can rekindle that relationship with them. As long as they are a good influence on you, it's worth it. Your life is meaningful and worthy of goodness. That not only includes someone to spend the rest of your life with, but it also includes your family and friends. Don't forget about your other loves in pursuit of the right one.

Continue to rewire your thoughts so that they will serve the best you. If you are still thinking negative things about yourself, even if it's once in a while, then you are not doing yourself any favors. Find that positive inner voice that speaks nothing but goodness into your life. Focus on that voice and amplify it until it's all you hear. Continue to find new ways of looking at things. Don't just see things as one point of view. This will broaden your horizon and make you more accepting of people and situations. This is such an endearing quality to have. People will admire it.

Find that love you desire within yourself first, and the rest will fall into place beautifully. It's such an empowering feeling to know that you don't rely on someone else to feel true love and acceptance. You will be okay no matter what. You don't have to have people pumping up your ego with compliments to make you feel good. You don't have to be perfect all the time. You can have a bad day and still feel loved. Understand how much power you have within. Anything you want, you can give to yourself. You don't have to depend on another person to bring you happiness or fulfillment. You will already have it. You will already have that perfect love, and when the right one comes along, they can share in it with you. It will not be two half-people trying to make it work. It will be two whole people who already had it going on. What an exciting love to experience.

If you are like many, you need someone around to hold you accountable for your actions. It may be a friend or family member, or maybe a coworker. If you have someone to hold you accountable and is serious about helping you grow, excellent! If you don't have someone around, or if you would like someone new, please consider my coaching. I love to see people grow and become their best selves. It's my passion to help people thrive in what they want. Their success is my success. If you are interested in my coaching, you can find me online. I want to help you find the joyful life you desire. A lot of the time, having someone who is not a friend or family member can help a lot. Just like a fitness coach, they only know you because you come to them for their services. They are unbiased about your situation and they are simply there to give you the tools and education you need to reach your goals. They can look at your situation as an outsider and more easily see what you need in your special circumstance. Doing it by yourself can be very difficult for some. Don't feel bad about needing help from someone. Having a designated person to hold you accountable helps rocket your success, as long as you take it seriously. Once you grow from this book, you can become a light for those around you. People will see the difference in you in more than one way. Instead of walking into a room and becoming a part of the negativity, you could walk in and change the whole atmosphere. People might start to see you as a joy to be around. Imagine how good that would feel – to bring happiness to your surroundings just by being there. It is possible. You can do it. You have everything you need already inside you right at this moment. The ball is in your court and your growth is your responsibility. This can be the turning point in your life you have been waiting for! It's up to you to make the decision and take it seriously. I believe in you.

If you need help through this process or maybe you need to speak to someone to help you make sense of it all, I hope you consider my services. You could grow so much easier if you had a helping hand. Sometimes you just need someone to pull you out of the mental clutter and shine a new light on the problems you are facing. Whatever you might need during this time, let me help. You will look back on yourself from a couple months ago and be surprised at how far you've come. Imagine how far you can go by this time next year, or maybe five years from now. Your potential is always growing. I'm so excited for this next chapter of your life! I hope you take time to journal your thoughts so that you can see your progress throughout time. It's interesting to read back through your old entries and see how different your mentality was back then. I hope you continue to grow and prosper into your greatest self. You are just as worthy as everyone else to have love and happiness. Give yourself the life you have always wanted. It's time to let yourself have it!

Chapter 12: Conclusion

"Why are you knocking at every door? Go, knock at the door of your own heart."

— Rumi

Well, you've finally reached the end. How do you feel? Can you tell the difference in the way you see yourself? Do you recognize new thought patterns and new ways of speaking to yourself? Do you wake up feeling like the world has more to offer? I hope you feel good about yourself right in this moment. I hope you have been taking the steps seriously and working hard to achieve the goals you set because you are absolutely worth the time and effort it takes.

Make sure you do all the steps completely. Don't be nonchalant about the steps you don't like. It's important you go through the process outlined in this book whole-heartedly. Work through the pain, think positively, understand your issues, rewire your old thought process, find a peaceful place to grow, find everything you need within, and keep practicing. Don't skip a step just because you feel like it's pointless – I promise it's not. All of these steps are imperative, and they work hand-in-hand. I don't want anything to happen that may cause you not to heal properly. You've been pushing your growth aside for far too long. It's time to do it once and for all.

Have you become the woman you envisioned yourself to be yet? If not, don't stress out. Just keep growing and working on your envisioned self every day. Hold her near and dear in your mind. Picture her in your daily life, in the space that you are right now. Know that she is completely attainable and she's waiting for you. She loves you just as much as you love her. Find a way every day to make it to her and one day it will happen. It may take a while, which is completely fine, but as long as you keep moving forward then don't stress out about the timeline. One day you will reach her, and you might not even realize it. You will just become her, and it will feel so natural. Then a few months later you may realize that you are finally the woman you were hoping to be all along, and it's such a happy feeling. Take time to love on yourself for all the hard work you have done. Be proud that you reached your goals. Realize how much stronger you are than you may have thought. You can be anyone you want to be. Spend some time in this period of congratulations and happiness, then start to create a new vision of yourself. Think about how you can continue to get better. Focus on what she looks like and start building on the woman you have become. Remember, never become stagnant. Always grow forward.

I hope you understand yourself on a whole new level now. Hopefully you truly know what has been causing the issues you've been having and can now move forward from them. I want you to know yourself better than anyone in the world. I want you to know the inner workings of your mind, your feelings, and your goals. Understand yourself better than anyone, that way when the right one comes along, they can understand you that deeply as well. They will know exactly what is okay and not okay with you. They can see how you expect to be treated and hopefully they will be able to help you grow in the life you desire. When you find this person, you will know that you found them because you were finally healed inside which created a safe space for them to be with you. You were giving yourself that love that you sought all along. You weren't expecting it from anyone else but you.

I am so proud of how far you've come. I'm sure it's been a difficult process for you, but you kept going and learned from it. You took your pain and made it work to your advantage. What an empowering thing to do! You did the work that the majority of people refuse to do. I'm sure it was messy and frustrating and possibly annoying at some points, but you kept moving forward. You are different from when you started. You will continue to change and get better. I just want you to understand the fact that you can be anyone you wish to be. You have so much power and potential inside of you that can launch you into all sort of different lifestyles. Your mind is where it all starts. If you want to be the CEO of a company or a famous musician, it all starts in your mind. Whatever it is that you desire, envision yourself in it. Keep thinking about yourself in that situation and then do the necessary work that will make you reach that goal. Speak it into existence. Have confidence in yourself that you can achieve it. You may have days where you feel like a failure and you might doubt yourself, but don't let yourself feel those emotions for very long. Keep telling yourself you are successful and have faith that you can make it happen. Surround yourself with people who will help you grow. Speak positively to yourself so that you aren't being counter-productive. You can do it! Keep working hard and believe in yourself.

You've given yourself completely to others for too long, it's time you take your heart back. No more wasting time on people who do not serve your greater purpose. No more negative self-talk and lack of self-respect. No more hoping someone will give you everything you want and need. No more ignoring your problems. This is your time to take back your life and make it what you want. You can absolutely do it. You are a warrior! Now you have the tools you need to launch you into the life you have been wishing for. Keep revisiting this book when needed to continue your growth process. Remember that you have everything you ever need already inside you. Just let yourself have it. You are an incredible human being and you deserve the best life. Be happy, loved, loving, and respected. This life will fly by, so make sure you give yourself the life you crave. I have faith in you. It's time to let your flower bloom.

About the Author

Mackenzie Nall has spent much of her life trying to find love in all the wrong places. She has been through a handful of toxic relationships and bad breakups. She couldn't figure out what was causing these patterns. Finally, she reached her breaking point in 2016 after the man she was committed to cheated on her with a coworker. She decided to spend a year alone so she could find the root of these issues and correct them once and for all. She did the work, overcame her heartbreak, and became the woman she wanted to be.

Mackenzie began working as a nurse in 2016. She moved to Canton, Georgia in 2018 and started a job at a drug and alcohol detox center. She recognized the same patterns in her clients that she used to fall into in her own relationships. Not only did she see them at her job, but many of her friends online would end one relationship on bad terms and begin a new relationship a few weeks later. Seeing these unhealthy habits prompted Mackenzie to write a book. In *Prescription for Getting Over Him*, she goes through the steps of getting over your heartbreak and how to find that love within yourself. Her book goes into detail about toxic relationships, breakups, how to work through the pain, and how to find that love you have been looking for. Mackenzie believes that if we would all take the time to work on ourselves and love ourselves first, then we could end this cycle of perpetual unhappiness.

Thank You!

Thank you so much! I can't tell you enough how much I appreciate you reading this book and taking the time to work on yourself. You are such an amazing person to try to better yourself. Just know that by you making yourself better, you are making the world a better place. I am so proud and so thankful to have you as a reader! You have helped my dreams come true by purchasing my book. I hope you share it with whoever you think will benefit from it.

I hope you continue growing. Check me out online on my website for more resources and supplemental material. Your growth process is so important, and it will always need tending to. I would love to be a part of it with you. I hope we keep in touch!

Made in the USA
Columbia, SC
21 January 2020